Leadership

Inspiring Others Through Authentic Actions

☑ **Inspire**
☑ **Influence**
☑ **Succeed**

Andrew K. Bolden

Disclaimer

This book has been written for information purposes only. Every effort has been made to make this book as complete and accurate as possible.

However, there may be mistakes in typography or content. Also, this book provides information only up to the publishing date. Therefore, this book should be used as a guide - not as the ultimate source.

The purpose of this book is to educate. The author and the publisher does not warrant that the information contained in this book is fully complete and shall not be responsible for any errors or omissions.

The author and publisher shall have neither liability nor responsibility to any person or entity with respect to any loss or damage caused or alleged to be caused directly or indirectly by this book.

Table of Contents

Introduction

The phrases management and leadership should be separated even though some individuals use them interchangeably.

In actuality, leaders of totally unstructured organizations are possible. However, managers, as they are understood here, can only exist when hierarchical structures define duties.

Separating management from leadership offers significant analytical benefits. It enables the study of leadership to be focused on without being constrained by prerequisites on management's more general problems.

To be clear, managing requires good leadership. One of the elements of being a good manager is having the capacity to lead effectively. However, a manager's ability to lead effectively also depends on their ability to do the other management duties effectively.

Managers must do all their job duties to integrate people and material resources to accomplish goals.

To do this, a defined function and some level of discretion or power must guide the manager's decisions.

Followership is the foundation of leadership. In other words, a person becomes a leader when others are eager to follow them. People also tend to follow individuals who they believe will help them fulfill their needs, goals, and desires.

Motivation and leadership are tightly related. Understanding motivation can help one better understand what individuals seek and why they behave the way they do.

Furthermore, via the organizational environment, they create, leaders have the power to not only react to the motives of their subordinates but also to stimulate or deflate them. Both of these elements are crucial to management and leadership.

Leadership may be characterized as encouraging others to work voluntarily and passionately toward accomplishing collective objectives.

People should ideally be encouraged to acquire a readiness to work that is accompanied by passion and confidence, in addition to a basic willingness to do so.

Does Leadership Fit You?

Leadership is an essential component of every culture. Any decent civilization needs someone to step forward and seize the reins.

We all agree that leadership is important, but does this imply that everyone is a leader? The truth is that some people aren't suited for leadership roles. They are adherents. Additionally, followers are as crucial to society as leaders. Where do you lie, then? Will you take on leadership responsibilities in your life?

Many individuals naturally have the impulse to assume such leadership positions. It simply so occurs that way. When necessary, they take the initiative. In the lesson, they speak out first. They seize control of the playground baseball game.

At work, they rise to the challenge. Even if you can't always be the first, those with leadership qualities are often seen and recognized throughout their lives.

However, not every leader is born with this ability. Many of them need to pick it up. Those who desire to lead may accomplish so by enrolling in programs and mastering the required leadership abilities.

Even if it all seems easy to understand, it may be difficult. Educating someone on how to respond to an unplanned event is difficult.

We often see those who put themselves out there to be picked, so to speak, for leadership positions because leaders are defined by their actions. This, however, is not always the case.

Leaders often take the initiative in emergencies

before anybody else does. When others are concerned, panicking, or are just in shock, these people will have a calm head about them and be able to recognize the important task ahead.

These individuals are most likely our society's real leaders.

Chapter 1

Leadership Is Action... Not Position

Good leadership gets people's attention! Period! It affects not just business but every part of our life.

A mother is a leader in the family, whereas a boy may be the team sport's captain or a daughter the debate team's captain. A group depends on the leader to guide them to success in practice. A genuine leader is highly moral, trustworthy, and regarded.

There are leaders and followers in our society. Are we destined for either from birth? No! Could you develop your leadership abilities? Absolutely!

All of these seem to be present in the leaders I admire:

- They have big ideas! They don't install a ceiling. Instead, there is no limit on how large or much better anything may be.

- The objectives are clearly defined, and attention is not diverted.
- All parties know the desired outcome; for instance, if you sell widgets, you must sell x widgets to become wealthy, or you want to win that football game and eventually the championship. Be aware of your goals.
- They can enforce instructions.
- When objectives are achieved, new ones are established, or the bar is raised.

If you are sincere, moral, consistent, and respectful toward them, others will voluntarily follow your example. It's always nice to provide praise when work is properly done.

In addition, a competent leader will remove a team member who repeatedly causes problems for the organization.

You may increase your regard for yourself and inspire others. What fantastic news!

Do You Lead Others or Slacker?

Do you consider yourself a leader in your industry or area of expertise?

I've discovered that many individuals who call themselves leaders are slackers, in my opinion. A slacker enjoys giving advice or assistance but does little to further their career or company.

Do you, someone in your up-line, or someone else fit this description? Team of the Minds?

Here are some suggestions that may be of assistance:

Leader: Praises and encourages the team.

Slacker: Quick to criticize and sluggish to offer compliments.

Leader: Has greater expectations for oneself or herself than for his or her team.

Slacker: Has great expectations for his or her

12

team yet fails to live up to them he/she should apply the same standard to themselves.

Leader: Sets an example for his or her team and leads by example.

Slacker: Blends in with the group and never assumes a leadership position.

Leader: Has a strong sense of ownership for the company and guides new colleagues as they progress (by studying the industry and overcoming challenges).

Slacker: Persuades someone to join his/her squad, then pushes them to the side or passes them off to someone else (referred to as "sign and drop").

Which of these qualities most accurately sums up you and your teammates? Be truthful to yourself.

Remember that a leader must guide and support others as they develop.

The same failure attitude will spread to his or her

colleagues if he or she lacks integrity and fails to act. A team will imitate its leader and imitate the activities of its leader.

One more time, would you rather be a leader or a Slacker?

Chapter 2

Fundamentals of Leadership

The concept of leadership—what it is, who practices it, and how to do it effectively—is surrounded by a dense fog of jargon, controversy, and spurious theories.

However, there are just a few things about leadership that a newly promoted person in charge of a group for the first time truly has to know.

A leader has been promoted and is responsible for a team's performance. But nothing spectacular happens to you. It will probably take you more than a year to settle into your new position.

Because your group treats you like a leader, you are one. What type of work you'll undertake is your sole option.

Your authority decreases as you get to the position of leadership. You just have to decide to work longer, harder, or smarter as an individual

15

contributor to enhance your performance. When you are in charge of group's performance; the group determines your fate. They decide whether or not to take action.

Your power increases if you assume leadership. Your subordinates pay close attention to your actions and words. They change their actions in accordance.

To accomplish a certain goal, you utilize your conduct (what you say and do) to influence the behavior of the individuals who work for you.

Your responsibility as a leader includes achieving the goal. Taking care of your employees is the other component.

Without concern for your employees, obtaining positive short-term outcomes can still be feasible. However, you need the voluntary participation of the greatest people you can find to achieve long-term success for yourself or your business.

Ultimately, you may evaluate your leadership

abilities using those two criteria. Did we succeed in our mission? Are my group members doing better now than they did yesterday?

In this book, Speak With Confidence: An Introduction To Becoming A Public Speaking Star By Captivating Your Audience, you can learn more about all this and do it very easily.

How to Become a Better Leader: The Blueprint for Leadership

A blueprint would be the first thing you would use to build a home. This blueprint is helpful since it offers more information than just home-building instructions. It further describes the completed home.

What relevance does this have to leadership, then?

Last month, I asked a group of leaders what they thought made a great leader.

In the following sequence, they responded:

A leader must be a good listener, enthusiastic, passionate, shows appreciation, a visionary, a role model, trustworthy, honest, organized, knowledgeable, credible, persuasive, charismatic, team-building, purpose-driven, problem-solving, and have the following qualities: patience, a willingness to act before having all the facts, consistency, understanding of followers, and the ability to adapt to change.

I'll add that the list I obtain from other audiences when I pose this question is roughly the same as this. This leads to some insightful conclusions.

- Take note of the items on the list, which are all related to the human aspect of leadership. That's fascinating since I often hear individuals downplay this aspect of leadership by using phrases like "soft" or "touchy-feely."

  Applying these qualities calls for more strength.

- The list eliminates traits like being strict,

mean, serious, impatient, vengeful, rough, furious, harsh, punishing, dominating, aggressive, or ruthless. This is true of other lists from other systems as well.

It's also noteworthy that many popular depictions of leadership strongly emphasize at least one of these "hard" traits. In actuality, individuals who lack the fortitude (or the abilities) to apply the human element of leadership seek shelter in these qualities.

- Who are you? Compared to the list of advantageous traits, how would you assess your leadership abilities? How would your subordinates rate your leadership if you were to ask them?

  Which traits from the "hard" or "soft" list would they list? Could you increase your effectiveness by enhancing any of those "soft" qualities? How about the other bosses in your company? Do they make the most of human potential?

People desire leaders who care about and treat them with civility and respect. They seek leaders who can boost their chances of success. They seek leaders who enthuse them with a vision of a better future and demonstrate how to get there.

Chapter 3

Leadership: Is Mentoring for You?

Here are some things to consider if you're thinking of mentoring a young kid.

Make sure mentoring is a good fit for you. Most successful mentors passionately love fostering the development of younger individuals. Before you start the procedure, be sure you'll love it.

Make sure you have the flexibility and time. You may think twice before signing up for a mentoring obligation if your calendar is full or you're feeling stressed out at home. Instead, wait until things are a bit less chaotic.

Make sure you are aware of the contributions you can make. While none of us are experts in everything, we are all excellent at something. Knowing your strengths and other potential contributions makes you more likely to succeed.

According to Jack Welch in his superb book

21

Winning, there are several right mentors; there isn't just one suitable mentor.

Thus, you are not required to complete every task. Your protégé should seek assistance from other sources than just you.

Ensure you know the kind of individuals you like working with and the ones you find challenging. The connection you have as a mentor should be enjoyable for both of you.

Be careful to be clear about what you want from your protégé. It's smart to let them know what you're counting on them to accomplish. A mentoring partnership must have clear expectations.

Ensure you know that a successful mentoring relationship should benefit both of you. Both of you ought to like it. You ought to both advance and expand. And you two ought to establish a lifelong acquaintance.

Mentoring may either be one of your life's most

fulfilling professional experiences or a time-consuming, unpleasant effort. Make sure you are aware of what you are entering.

Fulfill Your Potential

Over the years, the conversation, study, and argument around leadership and management have interested me.

The emphasis on the contrasts between management and leadership appears to be growing, and it seems to me that this has evolved in part due to deficiencies in either one or the other.

Most of us want to be powerful leaders or believe we already are. Developing and following a vision while persuading others to embrace the required transformations has some allure. True enough, nothing would change or become better if poor leadership didn't step up.

You may accomplish your company aspirations and reach your full potential with leadership training. Every successful business is built on strong leadership, and people management is a highly important ability always in demand.

You may get leadership training via open learning without being distracted by conventional study.

With open learning, you may complete the training course at the speed that works best for you while studying on your schedule and at your leisure. This means that regardless of family obligations, full-time work, or any other time restraints, you can simply fit your course around your present life commitments.

Through open learning, you may even get a respected business degree and expand your options for employment!

On the other hand, being a competent manager doesn't appear to be as appealing to many individuals. Maybe I'm interpreting the "climate" incorrectly, but management is often considered boring, monotonous, and filled with other "left-brain" activities that get little praise.

There seems to be a view that one may be a manager or a leader, but there doesn't seem to be much recognition that those skill sets can be present in the same person. This is false, in my opinion.

In my opinion, management, and leadership certainly need separate skill sets but must coexist for any transformation to be successful. It resembles a glove and a hand. Together, they create a fantastic team.

Chapter 4
Effective Public Speaking

Speaking in front of an audience is essentially a monologue, but one that is ready, able, and willing to listen to you as much as you want to learn from them.

Being heard would make public speaking more impactful. The following suggestions can help you stay in touch with your audience.

Greet them

You may take a stroll around the space before your scheduled speech to get to know the audience members.

Give a hearty welcome to the attendees when they arrive. Giving a speech to a group of individuals you consider friends is considerably simpler than doing it to a large gathering of strangers.

Be Positive

Sincerity says that others want and expect you to succeed. Audiences seek the best possible information, stimulation, and entertainment. They cringe together with you if you fail. Your audience will gain from your excellent speaking performance if you are successful.

There is absolutely nothing to regret

You risk drawing the audience's attention to the issue you are making an apology for if you admit to being anxious or apologize for any issues you believe your speech or delivery may have caused. They probably weren't aware of it until you brought it up, so you don't need to point it out to them. Be calm and quiet. Along with you, your audience will unwind.

Create Eye Contact

Engage your audience and come across as genuine. Better yet, try to seem as natural as possible while exercising moderation. The audience should be able to nod their heads in agreement with what you are attempting to say.

Do not ramble on in your speech. Particularly at the parts you wish to stress, pause for a bit. Additionally, this is an excellent opportunity to make eye contact with your audience and take a breather.

Never debate

You don't have to argue your position forcefully with someone in the crowd if they disagree with any aspect of your message during the question and answer portion of your speaking engagement.

A discussion is not only a pointless way to make your point, but it may as well never be settled. Get that audience member to talk to you after your speech, never before.

Relax Before Speaking in Public

The largest fear that the bulk of mankind seems tensely scared of, the dread of speaking in public, is second to the fear of death.

Forget about giving that presentation that might bring your business and your essential sales if you only think about anxiety.

Speaking in front of an audience and giving presentations are two of the most effective and efficient ways to promote your goods and services. Why prevent people from hearing about your goods or services?

If you're still nervous, do your best to concentrate on the many advantageous outcomes of giving that presentation. If you let that unneeded and irrelevant fear consume you, imagine all the clients, customers, and contacts you would miss out on seeing or interacting with.

While your pitch or presentation may only last 30 minutes, its long-term impacts might be significant.

If your fear is still holding you hostage, try the exercises below to help your body relax and be ready for whatever you have planned for your presentation. See who gains the most by transforming that negative energy into a good one.

Get Your Body Warm

Do you currently have heels on your shoes? If you are, kindly remove them right away. After that, get up. Try to stand with only one leg. Shake the leg that is raised above the ground. Repeat the motion while switching legs. By doing this, you are expelling the bad energy of worry from your body and sending it toward the ground.

Even though it can seem and sound so unbelievable, this truly works. Just so you know, actors do this as a warm-up before tackling any scene.

Hold out your hands and quickly shake them. Bring your hands to your sides and place them over your head. The same procedure again. By repeatedly doing this, you'll release tension in your hands and arms, making moving naturally during your presentation easier.

Relax the tense facial muscles that are present.

You might chew with excessive force to do this.

These exercises are performed to warm up any areas of your body that are cold from being too anxious about how well you will do during your presentation.

However, refrain from overthinking since this simply causes unneeded tension. Remain calm, and your audience will follow suit.

Chapter 5

The Real Costs Of Skipping Leadership Training

According to a study by the Said Business School at Oxford University in the UK, executive education programs for Britain's private and public sectors waste up to $140 million annually due to poor planning and execution.

According to the study's findings, 35% of HR directors and 21% of other executives said that their present training and development initiatives were reaching the strategic goals of their organizations.

Most of the funds were going toward specially created courses for top executives.

If they want to stop, I know where those companies can stop squandering money on ineffective management training. Additionally, it has nothing to do with hiring additional academics

32

to create unique programs, activities, and trips for senior employees.

Folks, here's a fresh thought. Why not invest your money in leadership development and training in the field where it will be most effective?

The majority of businesses don't do it nearly enough. Only 7% of training expenses in the US were allocated to frontline leaders in 2003, and most of those funds were used for administrative learning and preventative HR.

The truth is that frontline leaders get very little training overall and focus less on developing their leadership abilities. Perhaps businesses believe they are saving money by forgoing frontline leader training.

Indeed, a budget line item would not take money intended for the CEO's office or the executive dining room. But there are also "opportunity costs," or the price of not developing frontline leaders, as they are known in economics.

The potential cost of missed productivity is one factor. Effective frontline leadership increases productivity and morale.

The opportunity cost of wasted leadership is one factor. The majority of great firms' leaders are self-developed. If you need leadership from outside, you'll have to pay for recruiting and transition expenses.

The expense of litigation is the last consideration. Organizations with strong frontline leadership are less likely to be sued. Additionally, if the leaders have been doing their duties, the defense will be simpler if the business is sued over a supervisory concern.

What about your business? Develop your leaders, do you? Do you assist them in acquiring the abilities required to raise morale, increase output, and prevent legal action? The next time you examine the training budget, keep it in mind.

How Executive Coaching in One-on-One Can Benefit You

Does your business need a boost? Are sales down, morale down, and your leadership strategies no longer working? Now could be the ideal moment to research leadership coaching.

A quality executive coaching program has to provide you with more than simply a speaker who goes through a PowerPoint presentation.

When your senior executives are paired with an effective corporate coaching program, you may have conversations about cultivating connections, developing strategy, and enhancing revenue and communications while hitting the slopes, scaling a mountain, or rafting some white water.

In a setting where you may be creative, it's simple to connect, and consider novel ideas.

In your business, a strong leadership structure may make a huge impact. Communication, human performance, accountability, delivery, and assessment are some of their implications.

A personalized curriculum with one-on-one instruction, and the greatest option in executive coaching is to focus on the unique demands of the firm.

If you're interested in participating in an executive coaching program, there are a few key factors to consider. Choose a firm that will provide you with a speaker who is more than that.

As your company develops and undergoes change, you want to be connected with someone who will serve as a trusted counsel to you. A quality coaching program would also employ industry experts to provide knowledgeable counsel in a few technical areas.

Discuss with your consultant the objectives you want your leadership program to achieve. Every company or organization needs guidance in a distinct field or division.

The one-on-one coaching program is so special;

you focus on achieving objectives where your business most needs them.

Chapter 6
How To Unleash Your Full Leadership Potential

There is a constant flow of knowledge about "what is leadership" or "how to develop a leader" in the form of books, articles, white papers, and training.

I won't address those two queries in this issue, instead focusing on two others that I think many of you readers may have on your minds:

- Why does having superior leadership matter?
- How does stronger leadership bring about such changes?

Being a leader needs the synthesis of character, knowledge, and experience. It is a very special kind of human behavior. What can you do if you take charge and use your leadership potential? Modify the world.

Your path to realizing your leadership potential starts with a thorough awareness of yourself. Learn about your personality and they have to do with leadership. Knowing oneself better enables us to develop our leadership potential by maximizing our strengths and identifying our areas for improvement.

Following self-awareness and self-knowledge, you must improve your communication abilities. These don't only pertain to your public speaking abilities. This applies to both your verbal and nonverbal communication. Your ability to communicate effectively increases your capacity to strengthen interpersonal connections. The ability to learn is another crucial talent.

To determine how you and others you could lead learn best, consider several teaching strategies and learning preferences. This talent will substantially improve your capacity to make judgments and deliver clear directions.

An exceptional leader understands the importance of using team members' talents and skills, leading them toward increased productivity and effectiveness.

Therefore, leadership is neither a position nor a trait you are born with. You can learn to be a leader.

Dr. Ken Blanchard said the following regarding effective leaders in his book "The Heart of a Leader": "If you want to know why your people are not performing well, step up to the mirror and take a peek."

Effective Listening

All too often, we speak far more passionately than we listen. Yet, if we are to communicate successfully, it is essential.

Most relationship breakdowns are brought on by individuals talking at one another rather than establishing eye contact. The words are meaningless unless the listener picks up on the subtext.

We feel appreciated and are far more ready to negotiate and compromise when we are actively listened to.

There is much more to listening than just words. A significantly more reliable indicator of how someone is feeling than their words is often their face and body language.

You must actively listen if you want to be a good listener.

Here are some pointers for improving your listening skills:

- Establish eye contact.
- Study the talker's body language.
- Are they calm, tense, or furious?
- Extremes are simple, but the message is often considerably more nuanced.
- Mirror the speaker's body language quietly, dancing gently rather than making fun of them.
- Nod to indicate that you are paying attention, then respond appropriately.

- If you are unclear about their meaning, ask them to clarify by asking pertinent questions.
- Summarized so what your are saying is ….
- Use who, what, where, when, and other open-ended inquiries.
- When responding or asking inquiries, be mindful of your voice tone. It is much too simple to seem critical or like a member of the Spanish Inquisition conducting an interrogation.
- Apply empathy. Recognize challenges, but avoid telling examples from your own experience. The phrase "I sense that you are finding this rather difficult" is preferable to "Oh, I know, it happened to me, but mine was bigger, more difficult, etc."

Consider it seriously; if you are just going through the motions, people will be able to tell. Focus on the other person; leave your ego at the door.

Chapter 7

The Distinction Between a Leader and a Boss

Every boss is a leader. However, not every boss is a leader. This distinguishes between a leader and a boss.

There is just one main distinction between a boss and a leader. Due to their seniority, the boss is revered and followed.

A leader is admired and held up as an example not only because of their position of authority but also primarily because of their abilities and personal traits. Please use this reference while viewing these wallpapers.

Those who want to be leaders need to set a good example. The team must consistently have the conviction that the leader will be there in times of need.

To solve the issue, not the fault. The team

members will lose respect for the leader if they see that s/he does not practice what they teach. They could comply with him or her, but respect won't be shown. Leaders earn this esteem through their deeds. They search and behave honorably. Their words and deeds are perfectly in sync. They seem to have a consistent attitude and personality.

Every manager must exhibit qualities like knowledge, planning, anticipation, foresight, action, a result-oriented attitude, perspective, and respect for every team member and work to gain that respect and function as a friend and mentor.

This is a long list, but developing into a successful leader is necessary. This is true for individuals in all leadership roles across all organizations, not just those in national leadership positions.

A person transitions from being just a boss to being a leader after they get the respect of their team members.

Creating Leadership Characters

According to a self-help expert, leadership is just the capacity to make decisions.

The talents and abilities of other individuals are used to make things happen.

Many leaders undergo leadership development after being identified as having the potential to be a leader. However, others are extremely talented from birth.

What kind of sort of person makes the greatest leader?

Leadership Qualities

The most successful individual in charge of the biggest company or organization would also make the finest leader. There is a chance.

Could someone with a little drive or entrepreneurial abilities wind up on the other end of the pole as a leader? It's also conceivable.

45

Building Leadership Capabilities

Some individuals are very fortunate because they have an easier time developing their leadership talents than others. It is undeniable that certain personality types make better leaders than others.

What personality types would make better leaders is the next question. No matter how commonplace or odd our personalities are, they all fall into certain categories.

Regardless, it could have certain elements that would form a great sort of leader. However, your personality type could benefit greatly from training in leadership development and becoming a highly successful leader.

Despite their many differences, the following are some of the most identifiable leadership personalities.

Strong Leader

He is the organization's lion and its king. He fits

46

the bill for this.

Who wants to be the one behind the wheel?

Despite his quirky attitude, his leadership is strong because of his innate ability to make wise decisions. His propensity to be a morale-buster is a drawback.

However, people will gradually see his compassion and respect and adore him. Their growth and development may result from his struggles.

Leading Perfectionist

If he were an animal, he might be likened to a beaver in the organization. He will be the one to make sure that every "T" is crossed and every "I" is made.

This personality type is capable of handling every aspect of the group's everyday operations while letting the little things go. Another nice thing is that everyone he encounters will eventually pick up and use his knowledge.

Leader of Peace

He is a golden retriever and sometimes the most difficult to train. Most of the personality types described in any category may be frustrated by him.

He does, however, exhibit the greatest level of compassion. The others find it quite simple to express to him their deepest emotions.

Favorite Leader

Of all the other leader kinds, this one is the most entertaining. If there isn't any enjoyment, he will manufacture it for himself and everyone else.

His greatest asset is his ability to inspire everyone to work together to achieve the organization's objectives. Except for the perfectionist, almost everyone wants to be with him.

He often misses certain crucial facts in his attempt

48

to make things amusing. The perfectionist would want to believe this, at least.

You as the leader

What kind of leader would you be? What are your advantages and disadvantages? What would you desire if you were being trained and cultivated to be a leader?

Individual Leadership Development

Some individuals may be born with the ability to lead. But without leadership development, these abilities may not be improved, preventing leaders from reaching their full potential.

Individual and group leadership development are the main categories that describe leadership development today.

The first often focuses on a person's particular leadership qualities, while the second is more concerned with leadership as a whole.

Development is a process in which the local populace and workplace are engaged.

Building Your Leadership Capabilities

If you believe you can succeed as a leader, now could be the time to think about developing your leadership abilities independently. You must first identify the barriers to your leadership effectiveness to achieve it.

Some people have personal concerns and challenges, while others have difficulty comprehending and accepting specific circumstances.

You must: be able to go over these problems and become a better leader.

Forgive yourself and let the past go: According to experts, many individuals have the potential to be excellent leaders, but they are too attached to the past and unable to let go of their previous transgressions.

If you want to be a good leader, try to realize that certain things are beyond your control. Then you'll be able to forget about it and go on. This will be a reminder of your failure if all you do is keep thinking about the past.

And if you dwell on your failure, you'll fall into a never-ending loop of blaming yourself for actions you didn't truly choose to do.

Keep your dream alive: Being a leader is not an easy assignment, to begin with. You'd need to put in a lot of work and self-evaluation to realize your full potential as a leader.

People who wish to benefit from effective leadership in the future should start by having a dream that they can cling to.

Whatever that person's desire may be, large or small, it doesn't matter if they are prepared to do whatever it takes to make it a reality.

Some individuals are affected positively by great aspirations because they anticipate huge benefits in the future, which is why they are giving their all now.

Some individuals choose to have modest aspirations to ensure that they will be able to realize them and won't have to cope with disappointment or failure in the future.

Always think ahead: To build your leadership skills on your own, you must be able to inspire yourself to keep going in the face of several obstacles.

You may do this by planning and carrying out your tasks in advance, providing extra opportunities or chances if your first plan does not pan out.

Chapter 8

What Is Leadership Development

According to its definition, leadership development refers to any technique or endeavor intended to improve the standard of leadership in a person or the person in charge of an organization.

Traditionally, leadership development programs have been quite formal, severe, and inflexible because the individuals in charge of them want to make sure that everything formally takes place.

Before, only Masters in Business Administration (MBA)-style programs, which are often given at elite universities and business schools, were eligible for participation in leadership development events.

However, current trends in leadership development are moving toward a more relaxed and intimate environment. Even while it has a serious and professional tone, many of those who

53

lead it use additional strategies to encourage the attendees to actively participate in the sessions.

Action learning, which uses movements to teach leadership ideals, is one of the trends in leadership development today.

Others employ high-ropes, treks, and adventure courses to help participants unlock their inner leadership potential.

Others engage in executive retreats believing that these busy people need a calm and serene setting to think about their problems and, ideally, emerge as better people and leaders.

Types Of Leadership Development

Both individual and group settings may be used to apply leadership development. Traditional methods are often used in building individual leaders.

These often target a person's leadership skills and gauge their attitudes when managing others or an organization.

According to experts, certain individuals may have an intrinsic capacity to lead. Still, if that talent is not fostered and acknowledged early enough, it may eventually lose part of its efficacy.

People with natural leadership abilities must go through leadership development as soon as feasible to help them reach their maximum potential.

Individual leadership development, however, could be challenging at first because it can be challenging to cope with certain personality traits that often reduce a person's ability to lead effectively.

According to experts, a person must participate in institutionalized programs to solve problems and raise leadership skills to improve their leadership. However, people may strengthen their attention and perseverance in learning new things independently to improve their leadership abilities. In addition to cultivating one's leadership, there is another way to maximize a leader's potential: enlisting the aid of others.

Contrary to individual leadership development, which focuses on certain traits of a leader, like behavior, thought patterns, or emotions, collective leadership development concentrates on developing leadership.

This leadership development will focus on the leader's and team's interpersonal interactions, social influence process, and team dynamics.

The team's environment, including the workplace culture and social network connections inside and between its members, will also be a key emphasis.

The Crucial Elements Of Leadership Development

Not all individuals involved in leadership development know the requirements of various types of leaders.

They are unaware that some leaders rely on others

or experiences to sustain them while others depend on themselves to develop their leadership abilities.

If your organization undertakes leadership development, you should know that the conventional, formal method is no longer effective. Now, even leaders desire to learn opportunities based on experiences rather than just ideas and texts.

Since many customers choose unconventional approaches to leadership development, you must learn how to develop plans that will guarantee their satisfaction.

Incorporating the idea of self-motivation into leadership development is now one of the most popular and successful ways.

This is due to the widespread opinion among experts that leaders today need extensive contemplation and self-evaluation. The ability to motivate oneself is crucial for Leaders since it will enable them to identify both their strengths and limitations.

Leaders can keep doing what they are doing and even improve it if they know their abilities. On the other hand, being aware of one's flaws is crucial since it enables one to identify areas needing improvement.

If one is aware of their shortcomings, they may be able to use them to their advantage and become successful in the future.

You must thoroughly explain how it works to the participants if you want them to be open to employing self-motivation to build effective leadership qualities.

Make sure they comprehend that a good leader may put their mind to anything by being driven. Putting one's mind to anything will enable one to anticipate the outcomes of what one is striving towards.

Starting with short, easy activities is the next best advice you can provide participants in leadership development. While being a leader may come naturally to some people, it may be quite

58

challenging to do so effectively for others.

Ensure your participants realize that starting small and easy will allow them to achieve their objectives more quickly and easily.

They will be able to develop the self-confidence they will need to face future obstacles that are larger and bigger if basic objectives are established and accomplished thus early.

According to experts, leadership development is a crucial element for those who want to succeed in their life. This is crucial because it gives the individual freedom in deciding which courses to follow.

Leaders are allowed to direct or manage their own life via the principles taught throughout the activities, which will enable them to be the best people they want to be.

The Formula For Successful Leadership Development

The two types of leadership development are individual training and group training.

These days, more and more businesses seek the assistance of organizations that provide this sort of training since several studies demonstrate its value to the business's overall performance.

Everyone involved in leadership development training would agree that conventional methods of developing leaders' abilities may not always be successful. This is due to the significant changes in learning processes during the preceding years.

According to statistics, many businesses that want leadership development training use unconventional methods to help their staff members build their leadership abilities.

This is due to their additional belief that modern learners benefit from connecting to their own lives.

Getting Individual

The human element is the secret to successful leadership development training. Previously, training was often conducted in formal lectures by stiff instructors and was centered on ideas. But nowadays, many leadership development programs emphasize a more casual, less formal, and more personable methodology.

These days, physical activities like team-building sports are the most common setting for leadership development training. Others turn to more sedate choices like executive retreats to allow the executives to breathe fresh air and unwind from stress.

Being driven is the one notion that is always covered before experts assert that this one attribute is the basis for being an excellent leader in seminars that accompany leadership development training.

According to experts, leaders may make choices that will impact their lives and careers in the future via motivation.

Motivating the participants is often one of the primary highlights of most leadership development training since it is essential to the activity's success.

The trainers concentrate on inspiring leaders because they think this is the first step in helping them change their perspective on life. This is crucial because if one has an optimistic attitude toward life in general, one can overcome any challenges that may arise daily.

Additionally, a leader with an optimistic view of life can transform failures into triumphs by taking advantage of any opportunity that comes their way.

According to experts, one must first maintain a positive mindset to acquire a good view of life. Once a good outlook has been established, organizing your thoughts is simpler.
One must do a self-evaluation to identify both their strengths and faults if one wants to build a

good mindset.

Once they have all been discovered, it will be simpler to change the negative traits into positive ones and more likely to improve the favorable ones.

Although it may seem easy during leadership development training, many participants still struggle to achieve this due to various variables, including personality, upbringing, handling of stress, and ways of dealing with failure.

How a Leader Can See the Future

A leader has several hats to wear. Sometimes a leader has to be the one who renders the verdict. A team's leader may sometimes need to maintain order. Additionally, there are occasions when a leader must mediate conflicts.

However, one of the most crucial responsibilities of a good leader is the ability to predict the future. To put it another way, a leader has to foresee future issues and changes that the company will experience.

This is vitally essential since it will allow them to build a more robust company and weather any storm. Additionally, it will enable businesses to benefit from market shifts and develop rather than just survive.

What is your process, then?

Financial Simulation

Making use of financial modeling is one solution. This leadership technique may be used in various leadership situations, including running a family.

The basic premise is that you'll examine your organization's financial scenario and then attempt to forecast how it can evolve.

You will examine your expenses and revenue to do this. What number of clients do you have? What percentage of your sales is profit? What other expenses are you making? How soon will you finish repaying your debt?

This enables you to create a graph—your financial

64

model—on which you may base your future profit projections.

This might either be a gradual slope or a severe incline. It may take some time until you break even.

However, this knowledge now enables you to plan a budget by anticipating how much cash you'll have at any moment.

Additionally, it enables you to imagine hypothetical situations, such as how your company might do in the event of a rent rise. If the answer is "it wouldn't," you must adjust your calculations or make backup arrangements.

Resilience

A company must be resilient to withstand any changes.

There are various strategies to strengthen your company's resilience. Still, the greatest ones include the following:

- Adding new goods or income streams.
- Keeping cash on hand.
- Paying off any existing obligations and loans.

Chapter 9

Leadership Myths That Must Be Stop!

If you don't believe you are a "great leader" by nature, don't worry.

It's OK to think that there are others out there who are better equipped to hold leadership positions. Until we find ourselves in such positions, few think of ourselves as natural-born leaders.

The good news is that most leaders are created, not born, so you can learn the requisite abilities "on the job," so to speak. You're now doing research, a necessary part of this process.

Unfortunately, a lot of the information is incorrect, making things more difficult for us.

Some widely held fallacies about leadership do nothing more than lead us astray.

Here are some of the most awful...

Leadership Involves Shouting

One misconception is that being a leader entails "being in charge" and that doing so entails restraining their power. Yelling to correct individuals as required.

However, although this may have been the case in the 1950s, it is a completely outmoded strategy now. First, yelling just gives the impression that you are out of control and passionate rather than composed and composed.

Shouting further implies that you are in command of someone else, which you are not. You just find yourself in a situation where you can decide what to do next.

This is because of a contract that you and the person you are giving instructions have, and you have the right to end that contract at any moment. Even when they are not receptive to argument, respect individuals.

Leaders need to be 'One of the Guys'

However, trying to be "friends" with your team is unimportant. Although that could seem enticing, the truth is that it will just cause additional issues.

It makes it more difficult when you have to make difficult choices, it may invite charges that your private sentiments are interfering, and it sometimes verges on contempt. Be cordial, but try to keep work and pleasure distinct, at least in the workplace.

Being a Leader Requires Courage and Boldness

You don't have to be daring and bold to be a leader. It doesn't imply that you must possess limitless confidence, broad shoulders, or a large chest.

Since all leaders (except Optimus Prime) are also people, they all have shortcomings, character defects, and self-doubt. Being a leader is more about what you do than who you are.

How to Give Appropriate Directions

One of the key characteristics that will most strongly characterize you as a leader is how you delegate tasks. Since this will eventually account for the bulk of your employment duties!

As a leader, you will spend most of your time requesting others to do tasks and ensuring they are completed appropriately.

However, to accomplish this effectively, you must understand how to offer instructions and how to guarantee the greatest results.

What you must do is as follows:

Be Specific and Clear

Being clear and exact should be your first and most crucial priority. This is necessary since you must be able to avoid errors and misunderstandings.

If you offer unclear directions, your team will

either need to contact you for further information and clarity, or they may make errors that cause serious issues and might cost you money.

This implies that an effective leader is also an effective communicator by default. Train yourself to be a better communicator if you're not already one!

Explain the Why

However, what's even more crucial is that you provide reasons for the actions you're asking them to do. In reality, asking individuals to attain a given goal, explaining why, but not providing instructions on how is preferable.

As a result, you become a more detached leader and less of a micromanager. People enjoy this because it increases their sense of job satisfaction and trust.

However, focusing more on the what and why than the how can make your team adaptable as needed.

71

Say, for instance, that you instruct your team to print 500 flyers and distribute them across the area. What happens if the printers malfunction later? What if the roads are covered with snow? Your staff will either be lost or will approach you for guidance.

Instead, instruct your staff that 500 local ads must be placed. This now creates a wide range of backup plans and other possibilities. They may, for instance, hire a printing business to make the flyers, or they could utilize email or publicize them at the town hall.

In any case, by not needing your approval for every little change in the plan, they have completed the same task more quickly and satisfactorily!

How to Inspire and Motivate Your Team

Want to inspire your team to perform better and more quickly? So you should simply give them incentives for working more quickly and hard? Or suggest that those who take too long risk punishment? Wrong!

Penalties and incentives promote behavior more quickly, the shoddy effort that is more prone to result in errors. Furthermore, you promote stepping on one another to climb the ladder. You also inhibit originality!

What, then, do you do in its place?

Motivation: Intrinsic vs. Extrinsic

The issue is that both of these remedies depend on external drives. This indicates that the activity is not motivating in and of itself and that the motivation is coming from somewhere else. The crew will thus just want to complete it quickly so they can go!

On the other hand, if you can make the action itself rewarding, you'll find that people will naturally work more on their initiative.

So, how can one bring about this change?

Ownership

Giving your team some degree of control over what they are doing and giving them credit for their successes is one way to solve this problem. A viable strategy for doing that? It is to brand anything they produce with their name!

It makes students feel proud of their job, which is a key factor in why this works. As a result, the task is satisfying since it is their project.

If it succeeds, they will have something to boast about. And it will help them if they can boast about it.

Giving your staff some degree of control over their actions is also crucial at the same time. That entails ensuring that they can make choices and accept the associated responsibility.

Once again, this gives the project a stronger sense of being "theirs." and as a consequence, they are considerably more content to put in longer hours.

Of course, there are other ways to enjoy your job as well. Try it out! Introducing frequent breaks, altering the workspace, and even gamifying certain elements may significantly impact how your team functions and behaves.

Biggest Suggestion

The largest tip of all, though? Make sure your team is composed of the proper individuals from the start. Some folks will just not find your work fascinating. Additionally, they are not the right personnel for your company.

Conclusion

What characterizes a successful leader? Every leader is unique, of course.

Some leaders will be highly dynamic, outspoken, and prideful, while others will be quiet and composed.

Some people will adhere to the rules, while others will be inventive and flexible.
How they operate.

Although leaders come in a wide variety of forms and sizes, certain characteristics undoubtedly set them apart from one another.
Let's look at some qualities that make a great leader and some characteristics you should develop to lead more effectively.

Responsible

A good leader needs to be accountable. In other words, they must have the fortitude to take criticism when things go wrong and the bravery to take chances and accept them when those risks fail.

This is crucial because it guarantees that the team will feel comfortable and free to work to their full potential since they will only have to answer to one person who will look out for their interests.

Knowledgeable

Knowledgeable people make excellent leaders. Although no one is an expert at everything (and a good leader would be the first to acknowledge as much!), you should be familiar with the ins and outs of your field and line of work.

This is crucial because it will allow others to look to you for guidance when unsure of what to do. Additionally, it implies that you'll be able to comprehend the fundamentals of each aspect of your corporation.

You can monitor the wider picture and facilitate seamless teamwork across the board.

Calm

Being composed is crucial for a competent leader. This implies that you shouldn't yell at disrespectful employees and should never seem anxious, upset, or afraid.

A team's leader will always serve as a gauge of morale. The crew will begin to freak out as soon as you lose it. Even if you are anxious, be careful not to show it to others.

Passionate

A good leader should be very enthusiastic beyond all else. This implies that they should have a strong sense of purpose for what they're doing and an understanding of the 'why' behind their enterprise.

This is crucial because when you are enthusiastic about what you do and have faith in your company, you can motivate and encourage others. Without it, you'll just go through the motions, and the team will suffer.

About The Author

Andrew K. Bolden is a renowned Sales Acceleration Specialist with over 15 years of experience in sales and marketing. He is widely recognized for his ability to help sales organizations achieve peak performance fast by optimizing talent, leveraging training to cultivate high-performance sales culture, developing leadership and coaching skills, and applying more effective organizational design.

Andrew is passionate about empowering sales professionals to achieve their full potential, and he has worked with some of the world's most successful companies to help them achieve significant sales growth. He has a deep understanding of the sales process, and he has developed a range of innovative tools and strategies that have proven to be highly effective in accelerating sales growth and improving the overall performance of sales teams.

Other Books By Andrew K Bolden

- CUSTOMER RELATIONSHIP MARKETING: Effective CRM Techniques That Will Keep Your Customers Coming Back.
- EXCELLENT COACHING BUSINESS: BELIEVE IN YOUR COACHING SKILLS BUT NEVER STOP IMPROVING, LEARN TO BUILD A SUCCESSFUL ONLINE COACHING BUSINESS
- The Ultimate Sales Funnel: A Step By Step Guide On How To Build A Killer Online Business and Create Massive Amounts Of Wealth Starting Today
- Built For Duty: Claim Your Power, Live Fearlessly And Become Unstoppable To Win At Anything You Set Your Mind To.
- Unheard Ways To Achieve Greater PUBLIC SPEAKING: Master The Art To Speak Like Pro - Get Rid Of Social Anxiety And Become More Confident
- From An Idea To Reality: How To Handle Every ENTREPRENEUR Challenge With Ease Using These Tips
- Canyon Of Intellectual Being: Powerful Ways To Sharpen Your Brain
- Map To Success: 10 Simple Ways To Make Your Marketing Plan Successful
- THE FIVE R's: Your Basic Guide To Understand TIME MANAGEMENT, PROJECT MANAGEMENT, ATTENTIVE MANAGEMENT, EFFECTIVE ENVIRONMENT, SETTING GOALS, ORGANIZATION AND LEADERSHIP
- The Wealth Mindset: How Rich People Think and How You Can Too

LEADERSHIP

- The 6-Figure Blogger: A Step-by-Step Guide to Making Money Online
- Calm Your Mind And Grow Your Wealth: Understanding The Evolution Of Entrepreneurship And Building Leadership Skills To Succeed In Business
- From 9 to 5 To Your Own Boss: Building Your Dream Internet Business
- From Zero to Six Figures: The Ultimate Guide to Building a Profitable Coaching Program
- The Online Coaching Revolution: Create Profitable Courses, Books, and Videos to Earn Money While You Sleep
- INFLUENCER: Strategies, Tactics, and Secrets for Growing Your Online Influence and Monetizing Your Brand

One Last Thing...

Dear Reader,

I hope you enjoyed reading this book and found it to be valuable for your needs. As an author, it means a lot to me when readers take the time to leave a review on Amazon. Your feedback not only helps me improve my writing but also helps potential readers decide if this book is right for them.

If you have a few minutes to spare, I would greatly appreciate it if you could leave a review on Amazon. Your honest opinion can help other readers make informed decisions and can make a real difference in the success of this book.

To leave a review, simply search for the book title and my name on Amazon.com, and select the book from the search results. Once you have navigated to the book's page, scroll down to the review section and share your thoughts on the book.

Rest assured that every single review is personally read and appreciated by me. Your feedback is crucial in helping me understand what worked well and what could be improved upon in future editions. Thank you in advance for your support and for taking the time to leave a review.

Best regards,

Andrew K. Bolden